Hurricanes

MACMILLAN

Chris Oxlade

Macmillan Education
Between Towns Road, Oxford OX4 3PP
A division of Macmillan Publishers Limited
Companies and representatives throughout the world

ISBN 978-0-230-43235-2 [International edition]
ISBN 978-0-230-43067-9 [Spanish edition]

Text, design and illustration © Macmillan Publishers Limited 2013

Text written by Chris Oxlade

The author has asserted his rights to be identified as the author of this work in accordance with the Copyright, Design and Patents Act 1988.

First published 2013

All rights reserved; no part of this publication may be reproduced, stored in a retrieval system, transmitted in any form, or by any means, electronic, mechanical, photocopying, recording, or otherwise, without the prior written permission of the publishers.

Designed by Samantha Richiardi

The author and publishers would like to thank the following for permission to reproduce their photographic material:
Cover photography reproduced with the kind permission of Alamy/Marvin Dembinsky Photo Associates (satellite of hurricane), Corbis/Henry Romero/Reuters (people in hurricane); Shutterstock/B747 (palm trees).

The author and publishers would like to thank the following for permission to reproduce their photographic material: Top = t; Bottom = b; Centre = c; Left = l; Right = r

Alamy/Marvin Dembinsky p13(b), Alamy/Mary Evans Picture Library p19(b), Alamy/Kevin Howchin p28, Alamy/David R. Frazier pp36-37, Alamy/Ilene MacDonald p37t; Alamy/Borderlands p42(bl); Alamy/Jim West pp44-45; **Getty**/Mark Wilson p2(cl), Getty/MC1 Brandon Schulze p29(r), Getty/James Nielsen p3(c), Getty/Mark Wilson p(4), Getty/Stocktrek Images p6(t), Getty/Mike Theiss/NGS pp6-7, Getty/Mark Wilson p8, Getty/AFP p18, Getty/James Nielsen p30, Getty/Mehdi Fedouach p33(t), Getty/MC1 Brandon Schulze p33(b), Getty/Erik Simonsen p34, Getty/Joe Raedle p38(cl), Getty/Fox Photos p42(c), Getty/AFP p44(t), Getty/Mark Wilson p46(l), Getty/MC1 Brandon Schulze p46(r), Getty/James Nielsen p47(c); **Corbis**/Mike Theiss/Ultimate Chase p2(c), Corbis/Alberto Garcia p2(cr), Corbis/Eduardo Munoz/Reuters p3(l), Corbis/Michael Ainsworth p3(cr), Corbis/Bettman p3(r), Corbis/Mona Reeder p5(t), Corbis/U.S. Air Force p5(b), Corbis/Imaginechina; p9(cr), Corbis/Steve Brennan/epa p9(b), Corbis/NOAA/Zuma p15(t), Corbis/NOAA p15(b), Corbis/China Newsphoto p16, Corbis/Mike Theiss/Ultimate Chase p17(t), Corbis/Smiley N. Pool p19(t), Corbis p20, Corbis/Reuters p21(b), Corbis/Henry Romero/Reuters p22(t), Corbis/Henry Romero/Reuters p22(b), Corbis/Imaginechina p23, Corbis/Imaginechina p24, Corbis/Imaginechina p25(t), Corbis/Imaginechina p25(b), Corbis/Alberto Garcia p26, Corbis/Yann-Arthus Bertrand p27, Corbis/Jim Reed/Science Faction p29(t), Corbis/U.S. Coastguard p31, Corbis/David Bathgate p32(t), Corbis/Ed Darack p35(t), Corbis/Jim Edds p35(b), Corbis/Tim Johnson pp38-39, Corbis/Michael Ainsworth p39(t), Corbis/David Gard p40, Getty/David McNew p41(t), Corbis/Seaman Ash Severe U.S. Navy p41(b), Corbis/Tannen Maury/epa p42(tl), Corbis/Reuters p43(tl), Corbis/Bettman p43(b), Corbis/Pedro Ultreras/Demotix p42, Corbis/Mike Theiss/Ultimate Chase p46(cl), Corbis/Alberto Garcia p46(cr), Corbis/Eduardo Munoz/Reuters p47(l), Corbis/Michael Ainsworth p47(cr), Corbis/Bettmann p47(r); **NASA**/Visible Earth p10;
Shutterstock/Mamut Vision p29(b).

These materials may contain links for third party websites. We have no control over, and are not responsible for, the contents of such third party websites. Please use care when accessing them.

Although we have tried to trace and contact copyright holders before publication, in some cases this has not been possible. If contacted, we will be pleased to rectify any errors or omissions at the earliest opportunity.

Printed and bound in China

International edition
2016 2015 2014 2013
10 9 8 7 6 5 4 3 2 1

Spanish edition
2016 2015 2014 2013
10 9 8 7 6 5 4 3 2 1

Contents

A hurricane strikes	4	Mudslides on Pinatubo	26
What is a hurricane?	6	Storm surges	28
Where and when	8	Katrina's storm surge	30
The life cycle of a hurricane	10	Cyclones in Bangladesh	32
How hurricanes begin	12	Hurricane spotters	34
		Making predictions	36
The structure of a hurricane	14	Preparing for a hurricane	38
Hurricane winds	16	Surviving a hurricane	40
Wind damage	18	The worst hurricanes	42
Hurricane Andrew	20	Reducing the risk	44
Rain and floods	22	Glossary	46
Typhoon Morakot	24	Index	48

A hurricane strikes

'We grabbed a lady and pulled her out of the window, and then we swam with the current. It was terrifying. There were cars floating around us. We had to push them away when we were trying to swim.'

These were the words of a woman who lost her home when Hurricane Katrina hit the coast of the United States of America (USA) in August 2005.

Hurricane names
Weather experts have lists of names for hurricanes. They use a different list for each year. When a hurricane forms, it receives the next name on the list. If a hurricane is particularly damaging, such as Katrina, they never use that name again.

Residents of New Orleans stand in flooded streets in the days after Hurricane Katrina hit the city.

A New Orleans resident paddles through the flooded streets near his home.

Hurricane Katrina caused terrible **floods** in the city of New Orleans. Walls and earth banks called **levees** protect the city from the sea. When Hurricane Katrina hit, **sea levels** rose so high that water split over these levees. Water flooded three-quarters of the city, with only the roofs of houses left showing. Thousands of people in the city did not want to leave their homes, and some thought that they were safe. Sadly, more than 1,800 people died.

A member of a US Air Force rescue team looks for survivors in the flooded streets of New Orleans.

What is a hurricane?

A hurricane is a giant, spinning **storm**. A hurricane can be hundreds of kilometres across and more than ten kilometres high. Inside a hurricane are thick clouds, **thunderstorms** and heavy rain. There are also super-strong winds, which can blow at more than 250 kilometres per hour.

This **satellite** photograph shows the swirling clouds of a hurricane, seen from above.

A hurricane's strong winds create huge waves at sea. They also push up the surface of the sea into a bulge, called a **storm surge**. If a hurricane hits land, the winds destroy buildings and the storm surge floods the coast. A hurricane's heavy rain can also cause flooding.

Hurricane is the name for a huge storm in the Atlantic Ocean. In some parts of the world, hurricanes are called **typhoons**. In other places they are called **cyclones**.

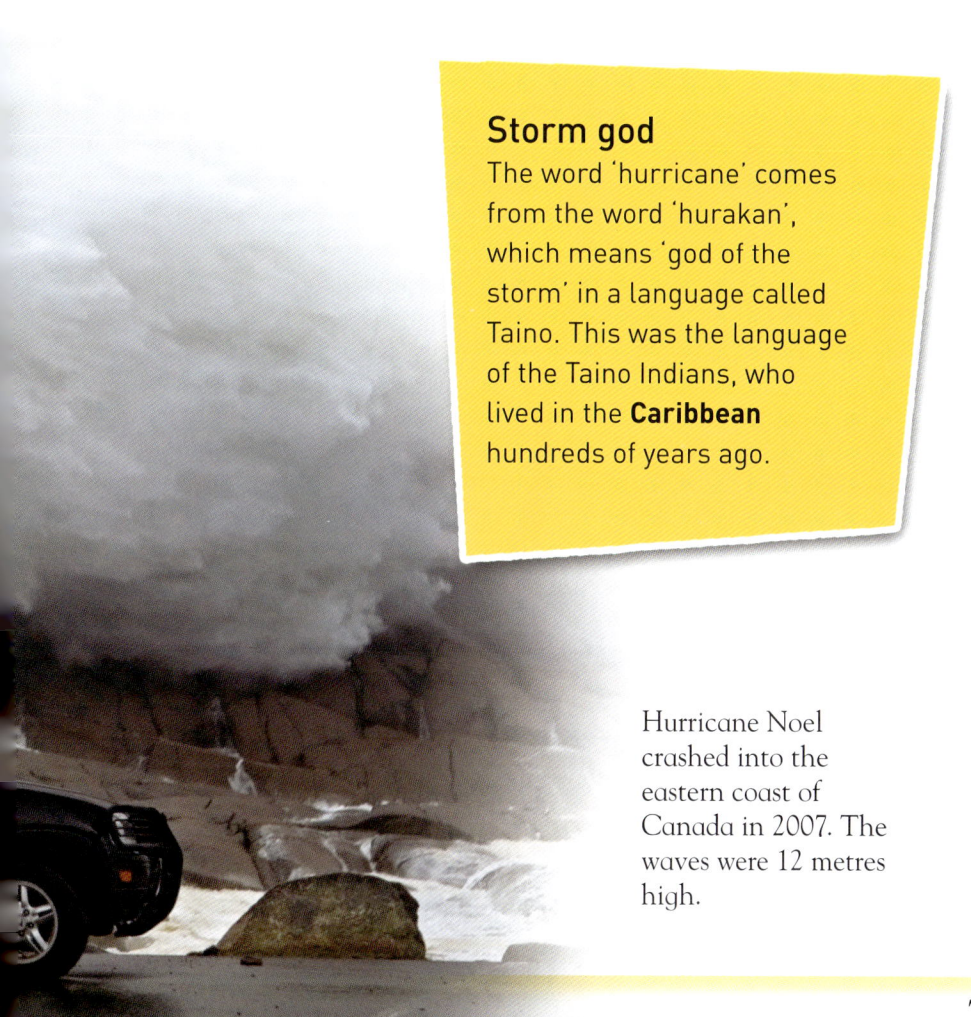

Storm god
The word 'hurricane' comes from the word 'hurakan', which means 'god of the storm' in a language called Taino. This was the language of the Taino Indians, who lived in the **Caribbean** hundreds of years ago.

Hurricane Noel crashed into the eastern coast of Canada in 2007. The waves were 12 metres high.

Where and when

Hurricanes only happen in some parts of the world, and they only happen during some months of the year. The time of year when hurricanes form is called the **hurricane season**. In the Atlantic Ocean, the hurricane season lasts from June to November.

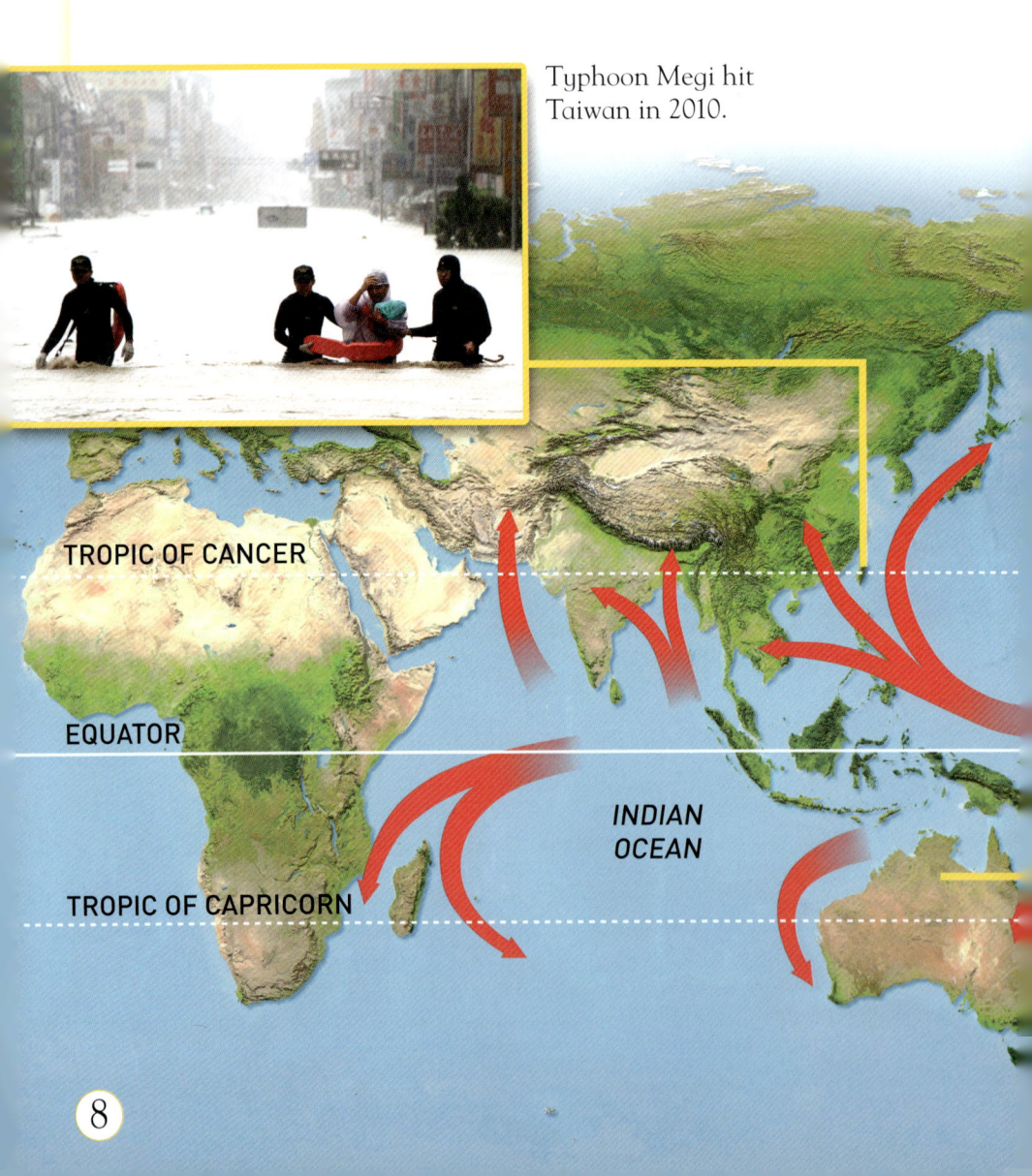

Typhoon Megi hit Taiwan in 2010.

TROPIC OF CANCER

EQUATOR

INDIAN OCEAN

TROPIC OF CAPRICORN

Hurricanes only happen in an area of the world called the **tropics**. This area is like a wide belt around the middle of the world. It covers the land and sea on both sides of the **Equator**.

The map below shows the places in the world where hurricanes happen. The arrows show where hurricanes start, near the Equator, the paths they follow across the sea, and where they hit land.

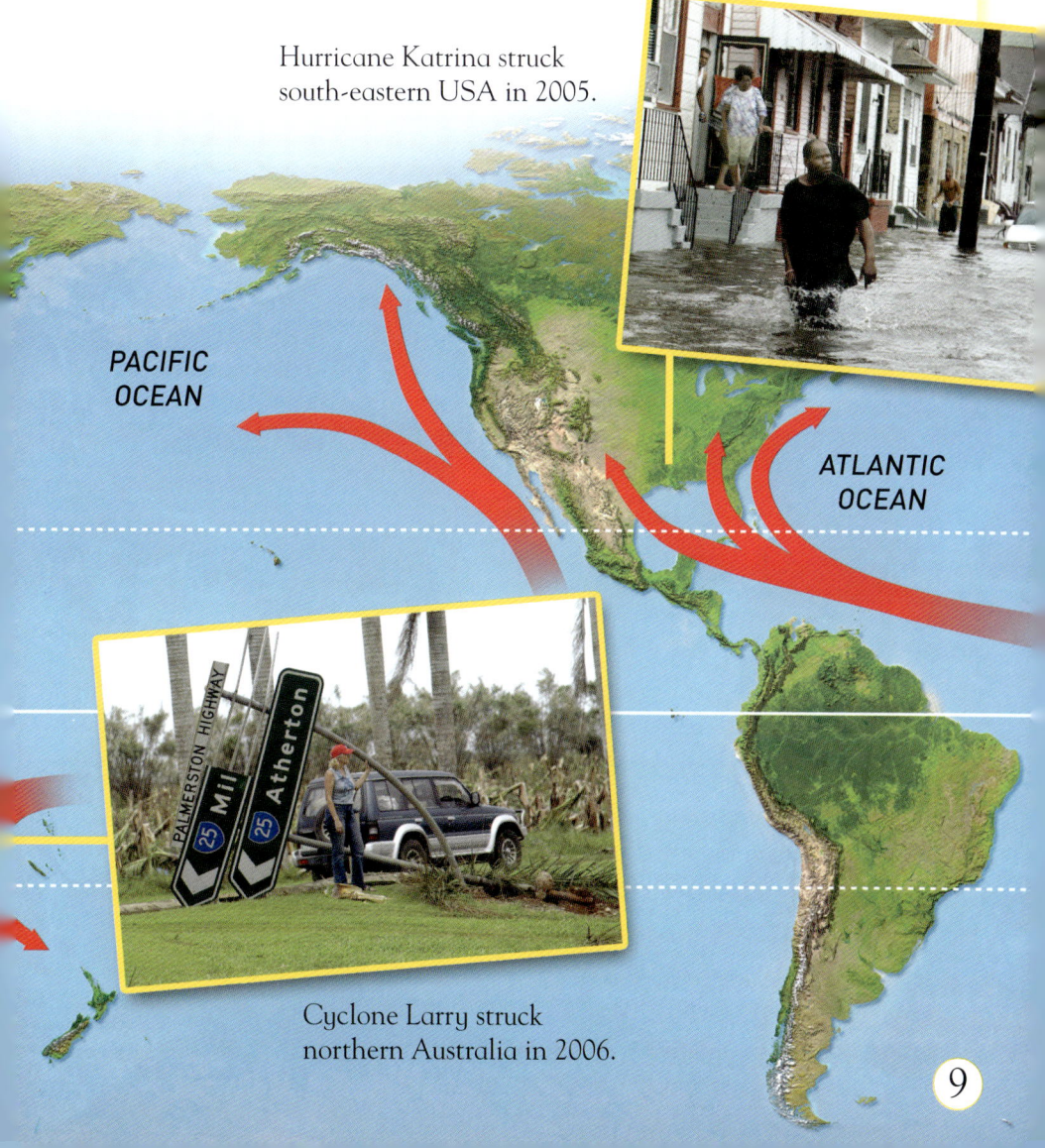

Hurricane Katrina struck south-eastern USA in 2005.

PACIFIC OCEAN

ATLANTIC OCEAN

Cyclone Larry struck northern Australia in 2006.

The life cycle of a hurricane

Every hurricane has a **life cycle**. It forms, grows in size, moves across the ocean for a few days or weeks, and then fades away.

1. A hurricane always begins its life cycle as a thunderstorm over a warm sea.

2. A group of thunderstorms sometimes turns into a spinning storm, called a **tropical storm**.

3. A tropical storm grows bigger and stronger. Eventually, it becomes a hurricane.

4. When a hurricane moves over land, or over cooler sea, it gets less energy. It slowly gets weaker, and its winds die down. Eventually it disappears.

Katrina's life cycle

Hurricane Katrina began near the Bahamas, on 23 August 2005. For a few days it was quite weak. But it grew much stronger as it moved over the warm waters of the Gulf of Mexico. It finally disappeared at the end of August, over the south of the USA.

1. 23 August: Katrina begins as a group of thunderstorms
2. 24 August: Katrina becomes a tropical storm
3. 27 August: Katrina becomes a hurricane
4. 29 August: Hurricane Katrina moves over New Orleans
5. 30 August: the hurricane becomes a tropical storm and begins to die down

How hurricanes begin

All hurricanes begin over warm seas near the Equator. Here, the temperature is always hot. Water **evaporates** from the warm sea, and turns to **water vapour** in the warm air. The warm air floats upwards, then cools down. When it cools, the water vapour turns back to liquid water and forms millions of tiny drops. These drops make up clouds. The clouds grow thicker and taller, until they are huge **thunderclouds** more than ten kilometres high.

1. A group of thunderstorms forms over tropical land or sea.

2. The storms pull warm air upwards, creating low pressure on the surface of the ocean.

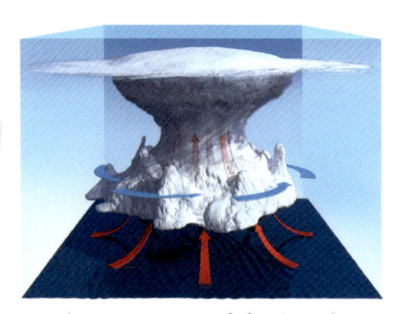

3. The spinning of the Earth causes the storm to rotate.

How many hurricanes?
On average there are 85 hurricanes and other tropical storms every year. Most of them are only small storms, and many disappear before they reach any land.

Thunderstorms are very common in the warm, moist air of the tropics.

Sometimes a group of thunderstorms begins to spin slowly. This happens because the Earth itself is spinning. They become a giant, swirling storm, called a tropical storm. Many tropical storms die away, but some get stronger and stronger. When the wind inside a tropical storm blows at more than 118 kilometres per hour, the storm is officially a hurricane.

This is a tropical storm called Alberto, which formed in the Caribbean Sea in 2006.

The structure of a hurricane

Hurricanes consist of bands of clouds spinning around a central point. They can grow to be truly enormous, with some hurricanes reaching hundreds of kilometres from one side to the other.

Right in the middle of a hurricane there is a round hole with no cloud. This is called the eye. Above the eye is clear blue sky.

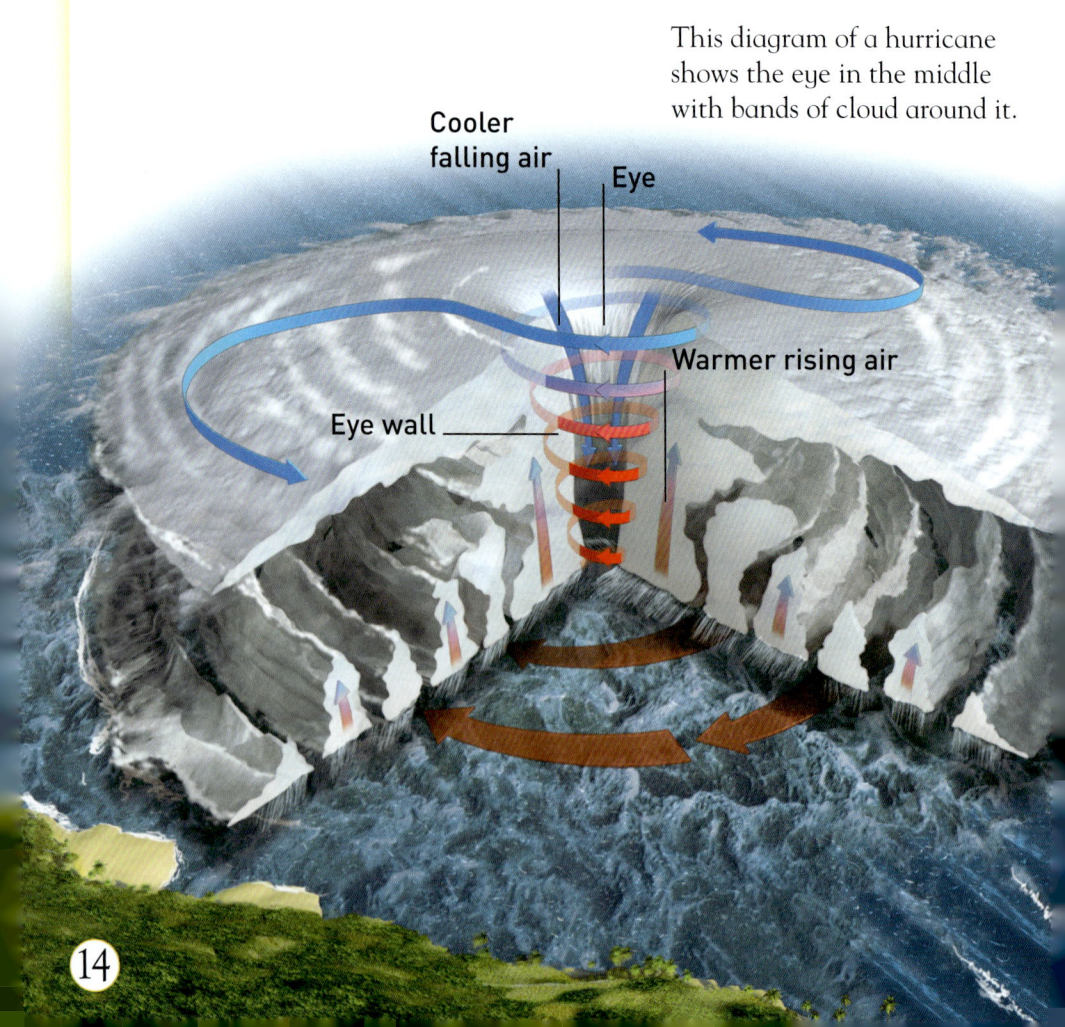

This diagram of a hurricane shows the eye in the middle with bands of cloud around it.

Cooler falling air

Eye

Warmer rising air

Eye wall

This satellite photo of Hurricane Katrina clearly shows the eye in the centre.

Normally the eye is about 50 kilometres across, but it can be as small as ten kilometres or as large as 200 kilometres across.

Around the eye is a bank of tall clouds, called the eye wall. This is where the strongest winds blow. In the eye itself the winds are calm.

The eye wall of Hurricane Katrina

Hurricane winds

Hurricanes bring very strong winds. Even the weakest hurricanes have winds which blow at more than 118 kilometres per hour. That means the air is moving as fast as a car travelling on a motorway. More powerful hurricanes have winds which reach average speeds of over 250 kilometres per hour. This is as fast as a high-speed train.

Thunderstorms around the eye of a hurricane can cause **tornadoes**. These can bring even stronger winds, which blow at up to 500 kilometres per hour.

People in eastern China struggle to stay upright in the fierce winds of Typhoon Haitang, in 2005.

As a hurricane approaches, the winds get stronger and stronger. But as the hurricane's eye passes overhead, the winds die away. This often makes people think the hurricane has gone, but then the winds get stronger again, and blow even more fiercely than before.

Hurricane winds tossed this aircraft into a tree.

Measuring hurricanes
Weather experts grade hurricanes from 1 to 5 according to their wind speed. The different categories cause different levels of damage when the storm reaches land. A Category 1 storm causes flooding and moderate damage. A Category 5 storm causes almost total destruction.

Category 1: wind speed 119–153km/h
Category 2: wind speed 154–177km/h
Category 3: wind speed 178–208km/h
Category 4: wind speed 209–251km/h
Category 5: wind speed over 252km/h

Wind damage

A hurricane's winds create big waves at sea and cause lots of damage when a hurricane hits land. When a hurricane's strong winds blow across the surface of the sea, they make waves. As the winds get stronger, the waves get bigger. The waves can be more than 25 metres high. That's as high as a seven-storey building. Waves this big can overturn and sink small boats, and damage big ships and oil platforms.

Hurricane Jimena hit the west coast of Mexico, in 2009.

When a hurricane hits land, the winds make a terrible screaming noise; they knock down trees and telegraph poles, and rip pieces off buildings. Debris, such as tree branches, roof tiles, street signs and garden furniture, flies around in the streets.

Winds from Hurricane Ivan caused this wall to fall into the street in Florida, USA, in 2004.

Divine winds
In the thirteenth century, Kublai Khan, the ruler of Mongolia and China, tried to invade Japan with huge fleets of ships. Typhoons hit the ships and badly damaged them. The Japanese thought that their gods had sent the typhoons to protect them, so they called the typhoons 'Kamikaze', which means 'divine wind'.

Hurricane Andrew

In August 1992, Hurricane Andrew hit Florida, in southern USA. Its winds caused terrible damage in the city of Miami.

Hurricane Andrew began on 17 August as a tropical storm in the middle of the Atlantic Ocean. At first, its winds were not very strong and **weather forecasters** were not too worried. But on 22 August its winds got stronger. It grew bigger and stronger so quickly that by the next day it was a Category 5 hurricane, with wind speeds of more than 240 kilometres per hour.

This combination of three satellite photographs shows how Hurricane Andrew moved across Florida.

'I was hiding in the closet. I'm telling you, I'm never living through one of those things again. I was just scared to death, scared to death, scared to death.'

Jim Bossick, who experienced Hurricane Andrew

A person struggles to walk in the winds of Hurricane Andrew.

Then, in the early hours of Monday 24 August, Hurricane Andrew hit Florida. The eye of the hurricane passed straight over the city of Miami. Strong winds destroyed more than 20,000 mobile homes and other buildings, and blew at more than 320 kilometres per hour. In all, 61 people died.

Hurricane Andrew's winds lifted this heavy lorry into the air and then dropped it onto a building.

Rain and floods

A hurricane carries billions of tonnes of water in its clouds. The water comes from the sea. It evaporates from the sea and forms drops of water that make up the clouds. When the hurricane moves over land, most of this water falls back to the ground as rain.

Heavy rain, dropped by Hurricane Wilma in 2005, caused floods in Mexico.

Rain from a hurricane can be very heavy. When it hits the ground it quickly fills streams and rivers, which can overflow in minutes, and flood the land on either side. These floods are called **flash floods**.

Rainfall from tropical storm Alpha in 2005, caused a flash flood in Haiti and destroyed many houses.

Heavy rain

A hurricane can drop as much rain in a few hours as normally falls in a whole year. When Typhoon Megi passed over Taiwan in 2010, nearly a metre of rain fell here in just 24 hours.

Rescue workers search the flooded streets of a city in Taiwan after Typhoon Megi struck the country in 2010.

Floodwater fills the streets with dirty water. It stops drains and sewers from working properly. Sometimes there is no clean water left to drink, which means that diseases can spread.

Typhoon Morakot

In 2009, torrential rain from Typhoon Morakot caused disastrous floods in Taiwan. The typhoon took a day to cross Taiwan. Its winds were not that strong, but the rain was very intense. Enough rain fell to cover the ground with water that was 2.8 metres deep in places.

Floods and **mudslides** washed away mountain villages, destroyed bridges and roads, and trapped thousands of people. A **landslide** of soaking wet earth wiped out the village of Hsiaolin (pronounced 'Sh-ow-lin'). In total, more than 500 people in Taiwan died as a result of Typhoon Morakot.

Rain from Typhoon Morakot made this river swell into a powerful torrent, and made buildings on the bank collapse.

'Standing at the spot where Hsiaolin village used to be, I could not see any man-made object: no building wreckage, no car parts, and no articles for daily use. All I saw were huge rocks, mud and driftwoods.'

Resident of Hsiaolin village, Taiwan

After Taiwan, Typhoon Morakot moved on to China, where about a million people had to leave as it approached. It caused more destruction, before it slowly died away.

A flooded street in China after Typhoon Morakot

Mudslides on Pinatubo

In 1991, in the Philippines, a **volcano** called Mount Pinatubo erupted at the same time as Typhoon Yunya arrived. Ash from the volcano mixed with rain from the typhoon, and created deadly mudslides.

Clouds of ash smothered the fields around Pinatubo in 1991.

First, Mount Pinatubo erupted with giant explosions. Millions of tonnes of ash blasted high into the air. The ash settled all over the volcano's sides and on the land around the volcano.

Then Typhoon Yunya arrived. Heavy rain from its giant clouds mixed with ash on the ground, and made thick, heavy mud. The mud flowed quickly down the volcano's slopes. It swept across farmland and into towns and villages. When the mud stopped, it set like concrete, and trapped everything in it. Most people had moved to safety because of the eruption, but they lost their homes and crops.

Quick mud
The mudslides that flowed from Mount Pinatubo reached speeds of 65 kilometres per hour. Some mudslides flowed 80 kilometres before they stopped.

Mudslides from Mount Pinatubo buried these houses.

Storm surges

As a hurricane moves across the sea, its winds push the water on the surface ahead of it. This makes a mound of water called a storm surge. The hurricane sucks the sea's surface upwards a little, making the storm surge higher still. A powerful hurricane can make a storm surge many metres high.

A hurricane's storm surge often does more damage than its winds and rain. If a hurricane reaches the shore, its storm surge raises the sea level at the shore. If the storm surge is high enough, the sea flows across the land at the coast. The water can flow many kilometres inland.

This storm surge has rushed up the St Lawrence river in Quebec, Canada.

A yacht lies in a car park near Fort Pierce, Florida. The storm surge of Hurricane Frances in September 2004 carried it there.

Huge waves can sweep inland, too, and make the flooding worse. A storm surge wrecks buildings on the coast, and carries boats and ships inland.

Animal dangers
During a storm surge, people can be at risk of attack from panic-stricken animals, such as snakes and alligators.

29

Katrina's storm surge

By the time Hurricane Katrina hit the south coast of the USA, its storm surge had grown to nearly nine metres high. The surge caused seawater to flood into towns and cities along the south coast of the USA, including New Orleans.

New Orleans lies on the Mississippi river and is next to a lake which connects to the sea. As Katrina approached, its storm surge made the sea level rise. This made the level of water in the Mississippi and the lake rise, too. Eventually water started flowing into the city.

Rescue workers pull a man from his home in a boat on the day that Hurricane Katrina hit New Orleans.

The authorities warned the people of New Orleans, but thousands of them decided to stay. Many people could not leave their houses and had to wait for days to be rescued. Along the coast, the storm surge rushed ashore and badly damaged the nearby cities of Gulfport and Biloxi.

Many roads in New Orleans became completely submerged in floodwater.

'My town is gone. The winds and waves have taken a once-great beachside town and totally washed it away.'

Resident of Gulfport

Cyclones in Bangladesh

Bangladesh is a country in South Asia. It has suffered many terrible disasters because of cyclones.

A lot of the countryside in Bangladesh is flat and only a few metres above the level of the sea. Along the coast there are many islands. Millions of people live in these low-lying areas. Most of these people are poor farmers, who live in simple homes of mud and straw.

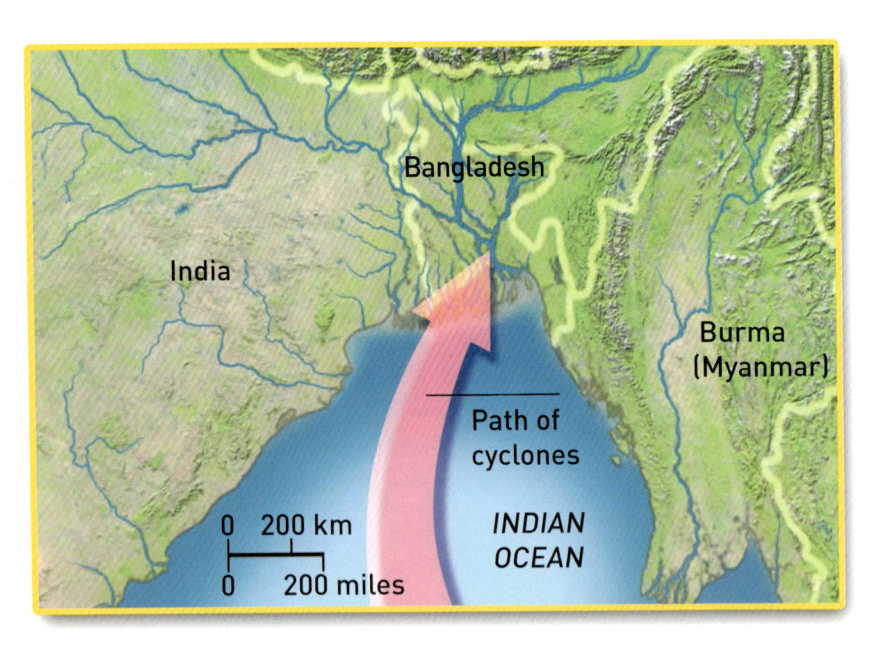

This is typical low-lying farmland in Bangladesh.

This map shows the route that cyclones normally take through the Indian Ocean as they approach Bangladesh.

Cyclone Sidr

Cyclone Sidr hit the coast of Bangladesh on 15 November 2007, with wind speeds of up to 260 kilometres per hour and a storm surge five metres high. It flattened buildings along the coast, and flooded cities, including the capital of Dhaka. Nearly 3,500 people lost their lives and half a million people lost their homes.

Cyclones often start their life cycles in the Indian Ocean, which is south of Bangladesh, and move north. Sometimes they hit the coast of Bangladesh. The storm surges from these cyclones sweep across the land, wash away homes and leave fields under water.

Hurricane spotters

About one-eighth of all the people in the world live in places where hurricanes can strike. They need to know if a hurricane is coming so that they can be prepared, or leave their homes. Expert weather forecasters watch out for new hurricanes all the time.

The forecasters look out for new tropical storms beginning over the ocean. Then they watch them to see if they grow into hurricanes. They watch how fast hurricanes move, and which way they are going, using satellite photographs. They also measure how fast the winds in hurricanes are blowing.

Weather satellites allow forecasters to watch the movements of hurricanes.

Flying through the eye of a hurricane

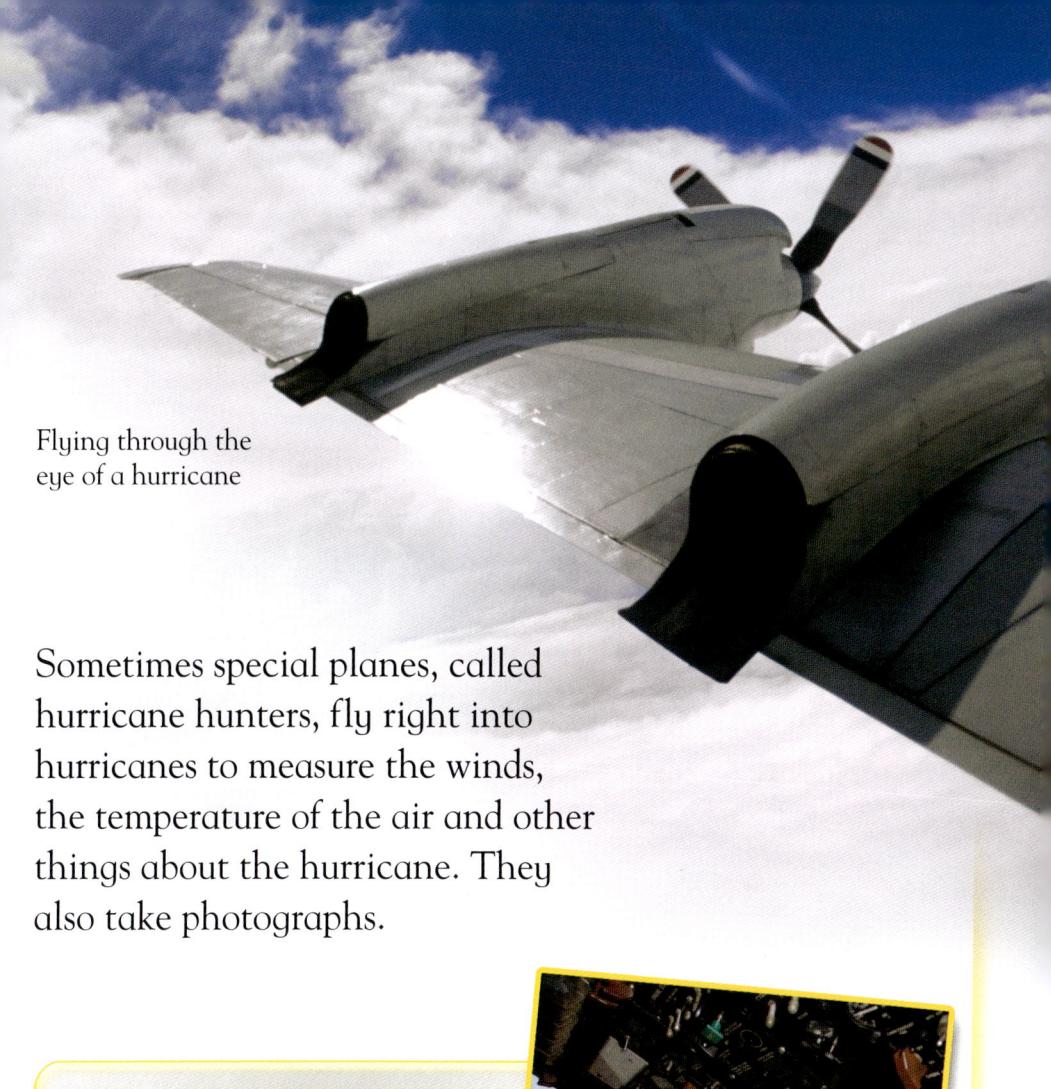

Sometimes special planes, called hurricane hunters, fly right into hurricanes to measure the winds, the temperature of the air and other things about the hurricane. They also take photographs.

Into the storm
Most pilots avoid flying into storms because they get a very bumpy ride, but hurricane hunters fly right through hurricanes!

Making predictions

When weather forecasters have all the information they need about a hurricane, they try to predict what the hurricane may do next.

Forecasters put all the information they have about a hurricane, such as its size and speed, and the strength of its winds into a powerful computer. The computer works out what may happen to the hurricane next – whether it may get stronger or weaker, and which way it may go. The forecasters also try to work out how high a hurricane's storm surge may be when it hits land.

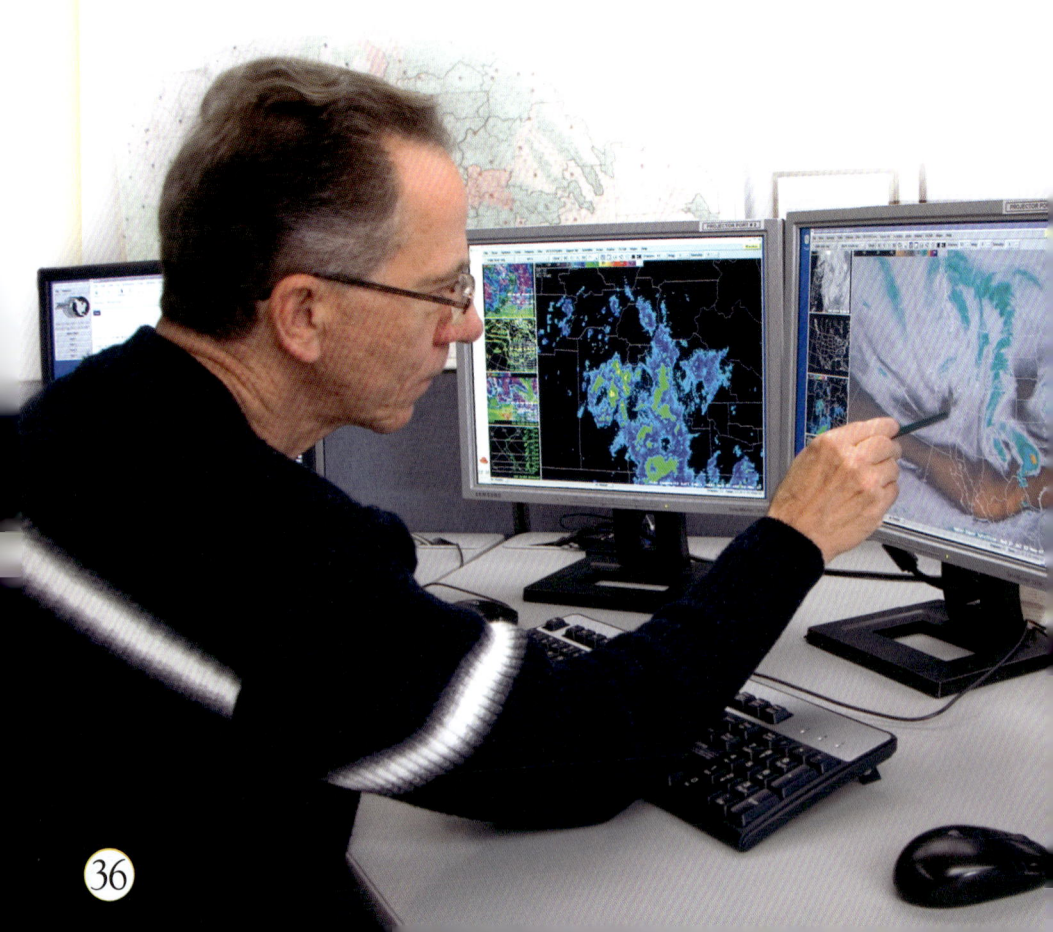

Regular weather updates appear on television when hurricanes are approaching.

When a hurricane approaches land, forecasters give hurricane warnings on television, radio and the Internet. The warnings try to make sure that people are ready if the hurricane does arrive.

Which way?
Hurricanes are quite unpredictable and they can change direction suddenly. This makes it hard for forecasters to say exactly when and where a hurricane may hit land until a few hours before it does.

A weather forecaster examines satellite images and weather data, which he can use to help make a forecast.

Preparing for a hurricane

When people know that a hurricane is coming they can prepare for its arrival. The first thing people need is a hurricane survival kit. This contains all the things they may need during a hurricane. A survival kit may contain food in cans, bottles of drinking water, a camping stove and pans, spare clothes, a first-aid kit, a torch and a radio. Shops often stock extra supplies of these items, ready to sell when a hurricane is on its way.

Shopping for emergency supplies

These men are boarding up windows in New Orleans before the arrival of Hurricane Katrina in 2005.

People also need to protect their homes and property. They need to put loose objects such as garden furniture indoors to stop them blowing about and causing damage. They also need to cover windows and doors with boards to stop windows breaking.

If forecasters are expecting a big storm surge, people need to leave their homes because there may be dangerous flooding. In big cities, millions of people may need to leave. There are normally special **evacuation** routes for people to follow in their cars. People without cars may have to leave in buses, or by train.

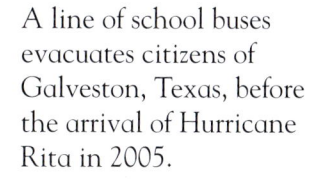

A line of school buses evacuates citizens of Galveston, Texas, before the arrival of Hurricane Rita in 2005.

Surviving a hurricane

As a hurricane approaches land, people need to find a **storm shelter** to keep safe from strong winds and flying debris. Some homes have their own storm shelters. There are also public storm shelters where people can go. These are often in local schools or sports centres.

Slowly the hurricane moves past. After a few hours, the winds begin to get weaker. Flood water slowly flows away as the sea level falls again and the rain stops.

Temporary beds fill the Louisiana Superdome, in New Orleans, which was the main hurricane shelter during Hurricane Katrina, in 2005.

These are temporary houses for people left without homes after Hurricane Katrina.

Once the hurricane has gone, it is time to clean up, pump away the floodwater, clear away debris from the streets and repair buildings. The many people who have lost their homes in the hurricane need help to rebuild their homes and communities. Poorer countries sometimes need **aid** from other countries.

Emergency supplies from the USA arrive in Bangladesh for the victims of Cyclone Sidr, in 2007.

The worst hurricanes

Here are some of the worst hurricanes, cyclones and typhoons that have happened in the world over the last hundred years.

1. Hurricane Katrina, 2005
This was the hurricane that did most damage in the USA. It cost between $100 billion and $200 billion to repair the damage.

2. Galveston hurricane of 1900
This was the deadliest hurricane to hit the USA. It was a Category 4 hurricane that hit the city of Galveston. Its storm surge washed right over the city, killing between 6,000 and 12,000 people.

3. Hurricane Mitch, 1998
This was the deadliest hurricane ever in the Atlantic Ocean. It killed about 18,000 people in the countries of Central America. Many people died in mudslides.

4. Great Labor Day Storm, 1935
This was the most powerful hurricane to hit the USA. It was a Category 5 hurricane that caused 423 deaths in Florida.

5. Typhoon Tip, 1979
This was the biggest tropical storm ever. It formed in the Pacific Ocean. At one point, Typhoon Tip was over 2,200 kilometres across, which is about half the width of the USA.

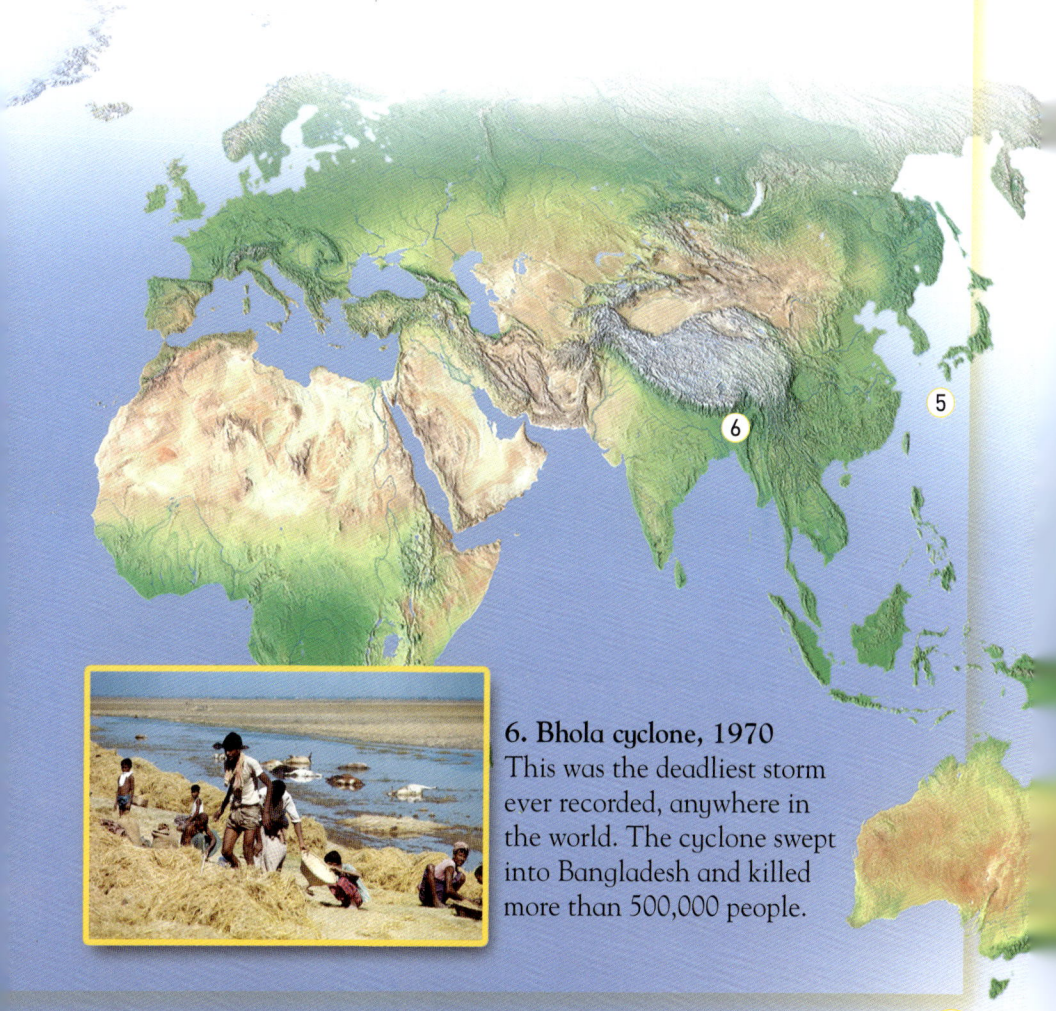

6. Bhola cyclone, 1970
This was the deadliest storm ever recorded, anywhere in the world. The cyclone swept into Bangladesh and killed more than 500,000 people.

43

Reducing the risk

This hurricane forecaster in the Philippines points to a satellite image of Typhoon Lupit, in 2009.

A hundred years ago, people did not understand hurricanes. They did not know a hurricane was coming until it arrived. Today, weather forecasters can see hurricanes coming days in advance. They can predict when and where hurricanes may hit land, so that they can warn people.

We can also deal with the dangers of hurricanes better. In places where hurricanes are common, people have action plans for when hurricanes are coming. There are organized evacuation routes, hurricane shelters, hurricane-proof hospitals, and **flood defences** against storm surges.

We now know much more about hurricanes, but we can still improve the way we protect ourselves from them. In 2005, Hurricane Katrina showed that severe hurricanes can badly hit even wealthy modern cities.

New homes like this one in New Orleans are on stilts to reduce the risk of damage from storm surges in the future.

This is a sign to a hurricane shelter in different languages in New York City, in preparation for Hurricane Irene, which hit the city in August 2011.

Glossary

aid help for a country after a disaster, including emergency supplies such as food and money

Caribbean the area of sea and the islands to the south-east of the USA

cyclone the name for a hurricane in the Indian Ocean

Equator an imaginary line around the middle of the Earth, the same distance from each of the Earth's poles

evacuation moving people away from danger

evaporate to turn from a liquid into a gas

flash flood a sudden flood that happens when intense rain makes a river burst its banks

flood when water from a river or the sea flows over land that is normally dry

flood defence a wall, bank or other barrier, designed to stop water flooding an area. A levee is a type of flood defence

floodwater water that has flooded over normally dry land

hurricane season the time of year when most hurricanes happen in a particular region

landslide when a hillside collapses, and earth and rock slides downwards

levee a type of flood defence, or raised structure, that helps prevent flooding

life cycle a series of stages through which something passes during its lifetime

mudslide mud that flows down a river or valley at high speed

satellite a spacecraft that orbits the Earth

sea level the average level of the sea's surface

storm a combination of strong winds and heavy rain or snow

storm shelter a strong building where people go for safety during a hurricane or other storm

storm surge the increase in sea level which often causes flooding when a hurricane reaches land

thundercloud a cloud that brings heavy rain, lightning and thunder

thunderstorm a storm with lightning and thunder

tornado a spinning column of air that sometimes forms over land, under a huge thunderstorm

tropical storm an intense storm that forms in the tropics, and sometimes grows into a hurricane

tropics a hot region of the world on both sides of the Equator

typhoon the name for a hurricane in the Pacific Ocean

volcano a mountain with a central crater where hot, molten rock comes out

water vapour the gas form of water

weather forecaster a scientist who predicts what the weather will be like

Index

aid 41
animals 29
Atlantic Ocean 7, 8, 20

Bangladesh 32–33, 41, 43
building damage 19, 22, 24, 33

Canada 7, 28
China 16, 25
clouds 12, 14–15, 22
Cyclone Sidr 33, 41
cyclones 7, 9, 32–33, 43

Equator 9, 12
evacuation 38–39, 45

floods 4–5, 7, 22–25, 28–31
Florida 19, 20–21, 29, 43

Galveston, Texas 39, 42

Hurricane Andrew 20–21
hurricane hunters 35
Hurricane Katrina 4–5, 9, 11, 15, 30–31, 39, 41, 42, 45
Hurricane Mitch 42
hurricane season 8

Indian Ocean 32–33

life cycle 10–11

Mexico 18, 22
Miami, Florida 20–21
mudslides 24, 26–27

New Orleans, Louisiana 4–5, 11, 30–31, 39, 40, 45

Pinatubo, Mount 26–27

rain 22–23, 24, 27

satellites 6, 34, 37
shelters 40, 45
ships and boats 18–19, 29
storm surges 7, 28–31, 33

Taiwan 8, 23, 24–25
thunderstorms 6, 10, 12–13
tornadoes 16
tropical storms 10, 13, 22, 34, 43
tropics 9, 13
Typhoon Megi 8, 23
Typhoon Morakot 24–25
Typhoon Tip 43
Typhoon Yunya 26–27
typhoons 7, 16, 19

waves 7, 18, 29
weather forecasters 34, 36–37, 44
winds 6–7, 15, 16–17, 18–19